TAXONOMY

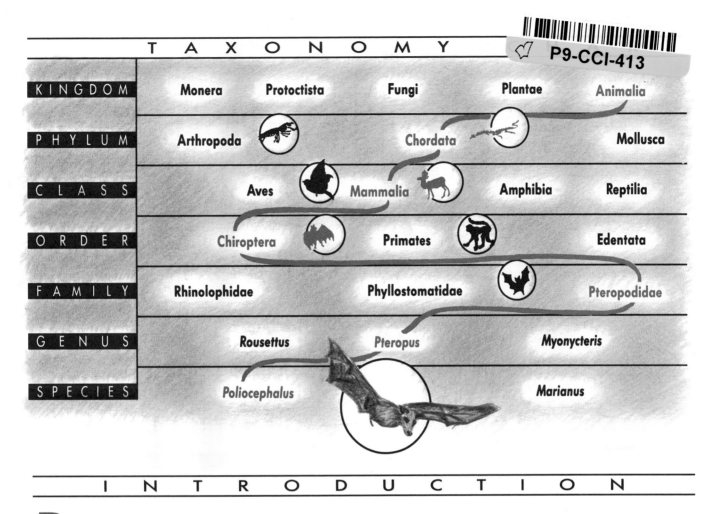

KINGDOM	Monera	Protoctista	Fungi	Plantae	Animalia
PHYLUM	Arthropoda		Chordata		Mollusca
CLASS	Aves	Mammalia		Amphibia	Reptilia
ORDER	Chiroptera	Primates			Edentata
FAMILY	Rhinolophidae	Phyllostomatidae			Pteropodidae
GENUS	*Rousettus*	*Pteropus*		*Myonycteris*	
SPECIES	*Poliocephalus*			*Marianus*	

INTRODUCTION

Bats are mammals. They share common characteristics with other mammals, including humans. All mammals have hair or fur, they nurse their young on milk, and they have a constant internal body temperature, which means they are homoiothermic. (Reptiles and amphibians, in contrast, depend on their outside environment for body heat.)

Lots of mammals jump and bound. Some can even swim. But bats stand out from the rest of their class because they are the world's only flying mammals. In fact, they can reach an air speed of more than 60 miles per hour and an altitude of 10,000 feet! Of course, not every kind of bat can do that. There are more than 900 bat species worldwide, so it's not surprising that these animals have specialized abilities. For instance, some bat species consume insects by the pound, others dine solely on fruit, and still others go for frogs, birds, and even fish.

Bats vary in size from the largest, the flying fox, which has a wingspan of more than 5 feet, to the most minuscule, the bumblebee bat, which is only 5 inches across with wings outstretched and weighs less than a dime.

Bats are extremely important in the balance of nature. Because they pollinate, reseed, and help control insect populations, you might call them nature's gardeners.

To keep track of bats and the millions of animal and plant species on earth, scientists use a universal system called taxonomy. Taxonomy starts with the 5 main (or broadest) groups of all living things, the kingdoms, and then divides those into the next group down—phylum, then class, order, family, genus, and, finally, species. Members of a *species* look similar, and they can reproduce with each other.

For an example of how taxonomy works, follow the highlighted lines above to see how the grey-headed flying fox is classified. In this book, the scientific name of each bat is listed next to the common name. The first word is the genus. The second word is the species.

Turn to the glossarized index at the back of this book of you're looking for a specific bat, or for special information (what's echolocation, for instance), or for the definition of a word you don't understand.

A Bat Tail Tale

To see the bat fly, flip the pages.

MEXICAN FREE-TAILED BAT *(Tadarida brasiliensis)*

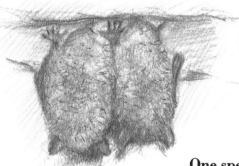

Photo, courtesy Merlin D. Tuttle, Bat Conservation Internat

He can climb vertical walls, he can hang from the ceiling, he can see in the dark, he can whizz through the air at speeds of 60 miles per hour. No, it's not Batman, it's a bat. With more than 900 species worldwide, bats are nature's super heroes!

One species of super navigators is the Mexican free-tailed bat. Each night at dusk, giant clouds of these bats emerge from their roosting caves in search of food. Their long, narrow wings are designed for speedy flight and endurance. They stay in the air almost all night long, bolting and darting in pursuit of insects. The largest groups can devour more than 500,000 pounds of insects each night. Take that, Batman!

Mexican free-tails do not hibernate. They stay active all year long. They leave the United States in the fall when the days are short and insects are scarce and winter in Mexico and South America where there's plenty to eat. In their travels, these bats can fly as high as 10,000 feet above the ground (where airplanes fly)!

Yes, Mexican free-tailed bats do have tails, and those tails extend freely beyond the tail membrane, possibly helping them to steer. These North American bats are sociable creatures, and they congregate in the largest colonies of mammals in the world. (Since adults only weigh a half-ounce—with a wingspan of twelve inches— they don't take up much space.) One cave in Texas is home to as many as 20 million bats at one time, each with more natural skills than Batman ever imagined.

Baby free-tails must learn to navigate inside very dark caves while thousands of other bats are jamming the air frequencies with echolocation signals. On its first flight, a young bat might travel 20 feet and avoid several collisions in one second, somersault in midair, and land on a vertical cave wall. Spectacular bat flights can be witnessed most summer evenings and mornings at Carlsbad Caverns National Park in southern New Mexico.

Newborn Mexican free-tailed bats roost separate from their mothers —upside down, side-by-side, sometimes as many as 500 babies per square foot.

Tourists are going batty at the Congress Avenue Bridge in Austin, Texas, which is home to the largest urban bat colony in North America. Between mid-March and early November, about 1.5 million Mexican free-tailed bats emerge at dusk from beneath the bridge and devour tens of thousands of pounds of insects nightly. Crevices underneath the bridge provide perfect homes for female bats to raise their young.

B A T S

BATS

Text by Sarah Lovett

John Muir Publications
Santa Fe, New Mexico

Hipposideros langi—head of adult male, showing nose-leaves and frontal sac (Neg. no. 103645; photo J. Kirschner; Courtesy Department Library Services, American Museum of Natural History)

Bats are mammals from the Order Chiroptera. Chiroptera means "hand-wing." A bat's wing has four fingers and a thumb just like a human hand. There are so many kinds of bats—almost one-quarter of all mammal species are bats —they form the second largest order of mammals. Bats have fur, nurse their young, and are warm-blooded like other mammals. Bats are the only mammals that actually fly.

John Muir Publications, P.O. Box 613, Santa Fe, New Mexico 87504

© 1991 by John Muir Publications
All rights reserved. Published 1991
Printed in the United States of America

Second edition. Second printing July 1997.

ISBN 1-56261-278-6

Extremely Weird Logo Art: Peter Aschwanden
Illustrations: Mary Sundstrom, Sally Blakemore
Design: Sally Blakemore
Typography: Copygraphics, Inc., Santa Fe, New Mexico
Printer: Burton & Mayer, Inc.

Distributed to the book trade by
Publishers Group West
Emeryville, California

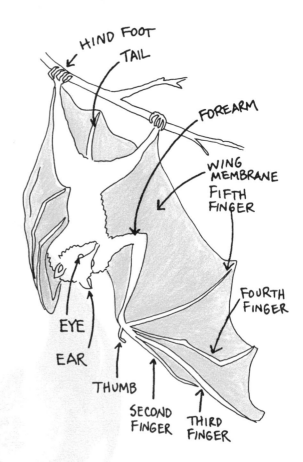

HIND FOOT
TAIL
FOREARM
WING MEMBRANE
FIFTH FINGER
FOURTH FINGER
EYE
EAR
THUMB
SECOND FINGER
THIRD FINGER

Very special thanks to Janet Debelak, Education Assistant, Bat Conservation International, and J. Scott Altenbach, Department of Biology, University of New Mexico

Cover photo, courtesy Merlin D. Tuttle, Bat Conservation International

Inside cover design from Neg. No. 2A 12069; Photo Jim Coxe; Courtesy Department Library Services, American Museum of Natural History.

Nuts about Fruit

Fruit bats hanging in a tree (Neg. no. 121314; Courtesy Department Library Services, American Museum of Natural History)

SHORT-TAILED FRUIT BAT *(Carollia perspicillata)*

Nuts about fruit, the short-tailed fruit bat lives in the rain forests of South and Central America where ripe cecropia fruit grow ready-to-eat. Fruit bats also love to munch on piper fruit the same way people eat corn on the cob. That's why they're often called piper-eating bats. Fruit bats are very important rain forest "farmers." As they fly, these bats scatter the seeds of fruit that will grow into trees and shrubs. In one night, a single short-tailed fruit bat can scatter 60,000 seeds. That's a lot of fruit!

Besides helping to keep rain forests healthy, these bats also replant areas that have been damaged by humans. It is fruit bats who carry and drop the seeds of hearty pioneer plants, the first to grow in areas of the rain forest that have been cleared. In fact, fruit bats are responsible for as much as 90 percent of new growth in cleared areas of tropical forests. Without bats, thousands of other plants and animals would surely disappear.

While fruit-eating bats scatter seeds that grow into new trees and shrubs, nectar-eating bats make sure plants will produce ripe fruit. Some fruit flowers need pollen from other flowers in order to produce fruit. Nectar-eating bats are attracted to the sugary nectar deep inside the flowers. As they feed on nectar, they become dusted with pollen. When they travel to the next flower to feed, they also drop off a little pollen dust, making sure plants will produce fruit.

FISHERMAN BAT *(Noctilio leporinus)*

The fisherman bat, a.k.a. the bulldog bat because its cheeky pouches give it a hang-dog look, catches fish on the fly. With ultra-sharp claws, very big feet, and long legs, this Latin American bat spears fish directly from the water. As soon as a fish is hooked, it is scooped into the bat's cheek pouches, where sharp teeth hold the slippery fish until mealtime. Fisherman bats stop at an available perch to eat, or they gobble on the go. A night's catch might be 30 or 40 small fish, crabs, and a variety of winged bugs. Although fisherman bats aren't particularly speedy, their wings are powerful enough to take them on nightly "fishing" trips. Flying in total darkness, they use echolocation (just like insect-eating bats) to detect ripples made by their prey near the surface of rivers, ocean lagoons, and the open sea. Fisherman bat "sonar" is so powerful, they can even detect a human hair poking a fraction of an inch out of water.

Bats are not blind, but at night they often use a system of navigation that works better than sight—it's called echolocation. Just like people, the bat makes a sound with its larynx by causing the air to vibrate. Most bat sounds are too high-pitched for the human ear to hear. The bat sends out pulse after pulse and listens for the echo as the sound bounces back from objects in its path. Scientists believe bats can "sound out" the difference between moths, mosquitoes, and other insects.

B A T S

GREY-HEADED FLYING FOX *(Pteropus poliocephalus)*

In the tropical forests of eastern Australia, the bats grow on trees. At least it looks that way! When 250,000 lively flying foxes hang out (and upside down) during the day in tree roosts, it's hard to tell the fruit from the bats. These roosting colonies get to be very noisy places, filled with the hubbub of a quarter million bats who squabble, chatter, and move from one spot to another (almost like a game of musical roosts). Indeed, standing underneath a bat-filled tree can be a messy experience because of all the bat droppings raining down.

When the sun sets, these foxy-looking bats follow their noses and eyes to apple, fig, and other fruit trees where they eat, rest, and digest food. Flying foxes use their mouths as "juicers" to squeeze pieces of fruit. They swallow the juice and spit out the seeds and pulp. In this way, seeds are scattered over nearby areas and new trees are planted.

Flying foxes have another "job" besides planting trees: they carry pollen from flower to flower as they feast on nectar. Grey-headed flying foxes are one of the most important pollinators of eucalyptus and other hardwood trees. This bat and its 63 known relatives are busy "gardening" all over the world.

In many parts of the world, flying foxes are responsible for re-seeding and maintaining rain forest diversity. Unfortunately, in spite of their importance to a healthy environment, many countries still allow hunters to kill vast numbers of these bats. Fortunately, some humans are beginning to appreciate how much these bats do for us. The people of southeastern Australia have created a preserve for flying foxes in the green valley of Ku-ring-gai. There, human "bat moms" learn how to care for orphaned and injured bats so they may be returned to the wild.

B A T S

LITTLE BROWN BAT *(Myotis lucifugus)*

One of the most common bats in Canada and the northern United States, little brown bats are lightweights—only one-quarter ounce!—and sport thick furry coats ranging in color from reddish to dark brown. Like all bats, they are extremely well groomed. Little browns mate in the fall and then hibernate all winter long in caves or abandoned mines. The sperm of little brown male bats hibernates, too. It stays inactive in the female's body until spring when her egg is fertilized.

Two months later, each female little brown bat gives birth to one baby bat that pulls itself out of its mother's womb. Although bat babies seem tiny to us, they are sometimes one-third the size of their mothers. The human equivalent would be an average-sized human mom giving birth to a 40-pound baby!

Little brown bats must grow up fast—almost within one month—and learn to hunt for insects. When the summer is over, they need enough stored body fat to sleep through the cold winter. Spelunkers (people who explore caves) must be very careful not to disturb colonies of little brown bats and other cave bats. When the bats are hibernating, they go without food, so they must conserve their energy and body fat. If they are disturbed, they fly. If they fly too often during hibernation, they may die from starvation.

MOTH EAR

MITES

Some moths have learned how to eavesdrop on bat sonar and take evasive action in flight. They hear bat sonar through ears on each side of their body. A tiny mite causes moths to go deaf when it lives as a parasite inside their ears. But the first mite to move in leaves a chemical trail for other mites to follow. The moth lives with one deaf ear and one good ear. In this way, the moth and the mites all avoid becoming dinner for a hungry bat.

Little brown bats form large nursery colonies during the spring and summer, sometimes choosing an abandoned building to set up housekeeping. People often accuse little brown bats of being a nuisance, but these bats hardly ever pose health problems to humans.

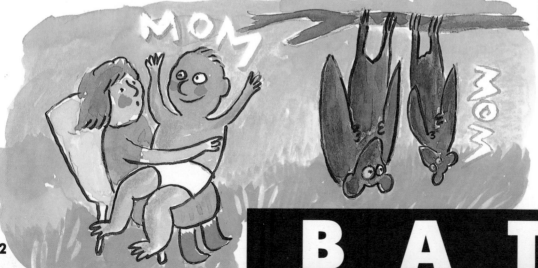

MOM

MOM

B A T S

FROG-EATING BAT *(Trachops cirrhosus)*

Flying on night missions, amazing frog-eating bats locate frogs by their call—they can also tell who's bite-sized and who's poisonous. These bats, living in the tropical forests from Mexico to southern Brazil, cause problems for male frogs—how to call for a mate but not a hungry bat.

Most bat hearing is adapted to the high-frequency signals used for echolocation. Frog-eating bats have another type of hearing—low-frequency—that picks up the loudest frog calls. These particular bats have developed this ability through evolution. As the bats slowly change, so do the frogs.

Frog-eating bats have encouraged frogs to learn new survival tactics. Some male frogs have developed mating calls that make it harder for bats (and female frogs) to locate them. Other frogs keep quiet on dark nights since they can't use their eyes to see, and frogs have no "sonar" to warn them of hungry bats.

Bats swim through the air with the greatest of ease. Well, actually they are the only mammals able to fly, but they use their wings to pull themselves through air, much like a swimmer "butterflies" through water. Bat bodies are featherweight, and their wings are made of two layers of skin stretched over bone. The bones in a bat's wing are the same as the bones in human hands, except bat fingers are extremely long. A bat's wings, ears, and nose are the only body parts not covered with fur.

BATS

Tiny, Flying Rhinoceros

LITTLE YELLOW-EARED BAT *(Vampyressa pusilla)*

With a head and body that is about as long as a human thumb and ears that are yellowish, the little yellow-eared bat lives up to its name. This bat's nose has a small horn that sticks straight up, giving it the look of a tiny, flying rhinoceros. Why do many bats have lumps, bumps, giant ears, and weird facial growths? Scientists believe these odd wrinkles help bats echolocate by directing outgoing and incoming sound waves. Most high-frequency sounds that bats use in echolocation can't be heard by the human ear, but we can hear some sociable sounds that bats use to communicate while roosting.

The little yellow-eared bat prefers humid areas of evergreen forests in southern Mexico, Peru, and parts of Brazil. It roosts in trees and shrubs and dines mostly on fresh fruit.

Bat detectors let you "see" bats with your ears. These instruments are designed to change high-pitched bat signals to sounds that humans can hear. With practice, listeners learn to decipher a "feeding buzz" from a "landing buzz" and the putt-like sound of big brown bats from the chirping call of hoary bats. All you need is patience and a city park to learn more about your neighborhood bats.

B A T S

Tutti Fruitti

JAMAICAN FRUIT-EATING BAT *(Artibeus jamaicensis)*

Latin American fruit-eating bats are nutty about mangoes, bananas, figs, avocados, and espave nuts. After dark, these bats carry small fruit to special places where they eat, but toward morning, they return to their regular roosts with a cargo of fresh fruit. It doesn't take long for fruit to pass through a hungry bat—only about 15 to 20 minutes. Scientists believe the fruit is digested with enzymes or chemicals, because there isn't enough time for bacteria to go into action. Fruit-eating bat droppings often smell like fruit, and these bats scatter piles of seeds, nuts, and fruit rinds beneath their roosting sites. In this way, they plant new fruit trees.

Female fruit-eaters give birth twice a year, probably because they have a breeding season that is longer than usual. Although a few species of bats commonly have twins and this is only once a year, most bats have only one baby per year. That means it takes a long time for bat populations to increase or recover from destruction.

Although bats live in most areas of the world, they are especially plentiful in the tropical forests. These forests are biological treasure chests containing more than 90% of *all* land-dwelling plant and animal species. They are also vital to the balance of our world climates. Making life choices that promote rain forest conservation is one way we can all ensure a healthy future for Planet Earth.

B A T S

A Day in the Life of Bats

WAHLBERG'S EPAULETED BAT *(Epomophorus wahlbergi)*

When she was eleven years old, Camellia Ibrahim began a log to keep track of a small colony of Wahlberg's epauleted bats that were sharing her house in Kenya, Africa. When Camellia wrote to Bat Conservation International for more information, she discovered that very little is known about these bats. Her journal shares firsthand observations with those of us who aren't lucky enough to have bats for roommates.

Camellia's Log I got up at 20 minutes to six so I could see the bats come in this morning. It was still quite dark, but our porch lamp showed them quite well. The scene under our eaves looked like a busy airport! The bats all used the same flight path. Some hovered to inspect roosting quarters and others had squeaky quarrels over territory.

March 8, 1987 There are 10 bats today. A mother and baby have a "room" all to themselves. The mother, Helen, holds the baby, which I have named Coffee, in her wings so you can only see the baby's head. She licks it often.

April 20 We have wondered how bats, hanging upside down

Reprinted with permission from BATS, BCI Vol. 6 (1), Spring 1988.

(or rightside down to them!), can make their toilet without dirtying themselves. Today we watched Tander do it. He used the extended thumb on his wings to hang on and let go with his feet. Then he turned the rest of his body down. When he finished, he brought his feet up again and let go with his wings.

May 7 28 adults and 1 baby. Fawn and Toto are still together, but Coffee has left his mother. He now roosts by himself, but still near his mother.

Bat Conservation International (BCI) can give you more information on bats. This nonprofit organization funds worldwide bat education and conservation projects. They also publish *BATS*, a newsletter for members of all ages. For a donation of any size, you can receive easy-to-follow bat house plans. Write to BCI at P.O. Box 162603, Austin, TX 78716.

B A T S

GOTHIC BAT *(Lonchorhina aurita)*

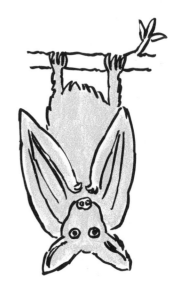

You might say it looks like a tiny cathedral, or maybe a stone gargoyle come to life. Either way, the reddish-brown Gothic bat has a very impressive sword-nose that is almost as long as its ears. From southern Mexico to Peru, Brazil, and Trinidad, this bat hangs out in caves and tunnels where the weather is humid and the trees are thick. And even with its fierce face, the Gothic bat is an easygoing critter.

Gothic bats often share their roosts with short-tailed fruit bats. As long as there is room in a tunnel for one group in front and the other in back, everyone seems happy. Occasionally, Gothic bats are loners who hang from trees and walls by themselves.

Bats spend most of their daytime lives roosting—that includes grooming, mating, raising babies, and socializing. Even at night, bats rest and digest at their roosting sites. Hibernating bats may roost for three months at a time. Besides caves, tunnels, and other dark places, bats sometimes choose to hang out in hollow trees, bushes, attics, and empty buildings. In fact, almost any nook or cranny will do for a tired bat.

A bat hang-out is really a bat hang-upside-down. Most bats roost by hanging from their toes, which lock into place when the bat's entire weight is suspended from them. Once "locked in," bats may fall asleep without danger of falling. Cave-dwelling bats also use their thumb-claws to anchor themselves to the ceiling. A few bats even have tiny suction cups on their wrists and feet to grip leaves and stems of plants. Bats' knees are on "backward," which helps them move around their roost.

B A T S

Photo, facing page courtesy Merlin D. Tuttle, Bat Conservation International

FALSE VAMPIRE BAT *(Vampyrum spectrum)*

People used to believe that the false vampire bat, from the tropical forests of Latin America, drank the blood of animals just like true vampire bats. Actually, this bat is one of a few bat species that are omnivorous (they eat meat, too). The false vampire bat lives on the flesh of small rodents, birds, and other bats as well as insects and fruit. When eating mice, false vampire bats chew the head first, the body second, and then throw out the tail.

This is a very big bat, as bats grow. It has a body length of about 5 inches and a wingspan of almost 3 feet.

Hollow tree trunks are the favorite roosting sites for small groups of false vampire bats, although they sometimes choose churches and other available buildings.

In scientific studies, captive false vampire bats are easy to tame and become very gentle. In fact, bats in general are surprisingly docile, shy, and easy to train. Of course, like all wild creatures, bats should be handled with care—and only by experts. Never try to capture a downed bat by yourself—it may be sick or injured.

Dracula, vampire, ghost, demon! Because bats hunt at night in complete darkness, superstitious people have long feared their "supernatural powers." As we learn more about the world, bats have revealed their gentle and beneficial nature, and "supernatural" powers have turned out to be extremely natural!

B A T S

EGYPTIAN FRUIT BAT *(Rousettus aegyptiacus)*

Shrill screams, hacking coughs, and the squabbling of bumper-to-bumper bats—this is the noise of Egyptian fruit bats roosting in ancient tombs and temples, trees, date palms, or caves. This might sound almost scary, but it's business as usual for fruit bats in Turkey, Pakistan, Egypt, and most of Africa south of the Sahara Desert. From their day roosts, Egyptian fruit bats probably travel small distances at night to find plenty of fruit juice and flower nectar, their favorite feast.

Because fruit bats poke their noses into flowers, they pick up and deliver pollen from one tree to another. While feeding, they are also making sure the plant produces fruit and seeds so there will be new plants in the following years.

Egyptian fruit bats mate from June through September, and females give birth four months later. Newborn babies are carried by their mothers until they're old enough to be left behind in the roost. Within three or four months, young Egyptian fruit bats can navigate on their own.

Egyptian fruit bats are important pollinators of the baobab flower. So many animals depend on the baobob tree for food and shelter that it is also called "the tree of life." If not for the fruit bat, these trees might disappear, triggering a chain of related extinctions.

While early American and European artists often painted bats as devils and demons, Chinese art is filled with lucky, healthy, blissful bats. Ancient Chinese scholars thought bats lived to old age because "they swallowed their breath" in deep dark caves. Artists in China still use five bats to represent five blessings: health, long life, prosperity, love of virtue, and a peaceful death.

B A T S

CHAPIN'S FREE-TAILED BAT *(Tadarida chapini)*

Chapin's free-tails (from Africa) are especially known for their "hairdos." Male Chapin's bats sport a flashy two-colored crest between their ears, but females are plainer and do without punk locks. This difference between the sexes is not unusual in bats and other animals.

Like male bats of many species, male Chapin's bats have specialized scent glands that are used as mating signals to attract females. These scent glands are located underneath the handsome crest, and the hairs help spread the sexy odor. Of course, it won't smell like cologne to our human noses, but the musk scent is bat perfume. Many species of flying foxes also use this technique, including the straw-colored flying fox, which has a rusty orange-colored patch of fur on its throat just above a scent gland.

Winter puts the skinny on bats. During months of hibernating, body fat keeps bats warm and nourished. As fat gets used up, a bat's body will shrink until it loses almost one-third its body weight!

Bat mothers give birth hanging upside down! Babies are tiny, naked, wrinkled, and born with a full set of teeth. Their itsy bitsy teeth are hook-shaped to stick tight to their mother's nipples.

Bats are worldly creatures. They live on every continent except Antarctica.

BATS

KITTI'S HOG-NOSED BAT *(Craseonycteris thonglongyai)*

This teensy bat, named for its Miss Piggy nose, is the smallest bat in Thailand as well as one of the smallest mammals in the entire world!

Because the hog-nosed bat is only the size of a large bumblebee, it's also called the bumblebee bat.

Hog-nosed bats, insect-eating cave-dwellers, are now endangered, probably because their roosting and feeding areas are being damaged by humans. In the area where the hog-nosed bat lives, many trees and plants have been cut down.

These tiny bats, which fit into the palm of your hand, need the help of conservationists to survive environmental hazards caused by humans. Although hog-nosed bats are found only in Thailand, conservationists from all over the world are working to save this very special bat.

Who's endangered? Every year, the International Union for the Conservation of Nature (IUCN) updates its list of endangered plant and animal species worldwide. Scientists believe that many species not on the endangered list should be. Unfortunately, some bat species are so shy they are rarely seen by humans and very little is known about them. No one even knows if they're endangered!

Assorted sizes. The tiniest bat is Kitti's hog-nosed with a wingspan of 5½ inches. The biggest bat is a flying fox with a wing spread of 5½ feet!

Bumblebee bat bodies are about the size of a jelly bean or a hazelnut, and they weigh less than a dime!

B A T S

This glossarized index will help you find specific information and understand the meaning of some of the words used in this book.

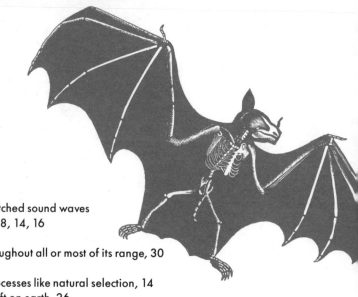